Reflections

www.MyColorBooks.com

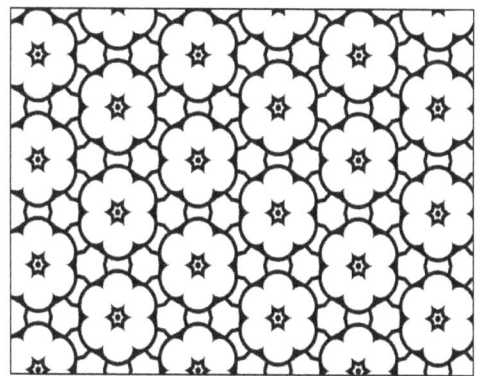

MandaLove Press

Copyright © 2015 by Creative Coloring Books for Adults. All Rights Reserved.

www.MyColorBooks.com

www.Facebook.com/CreativeColoringBooks

Published by MandaLove Press, LLC

First Edition Printed November 2015

ISBN-13:978-0692559543

ISBN-10:069255954X

Printed in the United States of America

Distributed by Adult Coloring Book Creative

Hours of fun and relaxation inside ...

REFLECTIONS is one of our favorite coloring books. We had a lot of fun creating this wonderful collection of 50 repeating pattern pages. Every single page of **REFLECTIONS** has a design we love, and we know you'll love **REFLECTIONS**, too!

Take **REFLECTIONS** home with you today. Curl up in your favorite chair, pick a page out of the book that strikes your fancy, and color. **REFLECTIONS** is filled with many hours of relaxing, quiet time for you, and hours of creative fun for the entire family,

REFLECTIONS contains an intriguing mix of original, one-of-a-kind repeating pattern pages. The design styles range from easy to complex. With 50 designs to choose from, each member of the family can easily find a coloring page that sparks their imagination and inspires their inner artist.

The designs in **REFLECTIONS** are printed one to a page, but markers can bleed through even the best paper. Two blotter pages have been added to the back of the book for you to use to keep your artwork pristine.

Free coloring pages ...

Subscribe to our newsletter today and we'll send you a free set of bonus mandalas to color. You'll also have a chance to win a brand new coloring book!

We choose a new winner every month: **http://www.MandaLovePress.com**

Join us on Facebook and you'll have access to free coloring pages and more chances to win free coloring supplies and coloring books:
https://www.Facebook.com/CreativeColoringBooks

Look for our coloring books on Amazon and at your local bookstore!

Thank you for supporting independent artists!

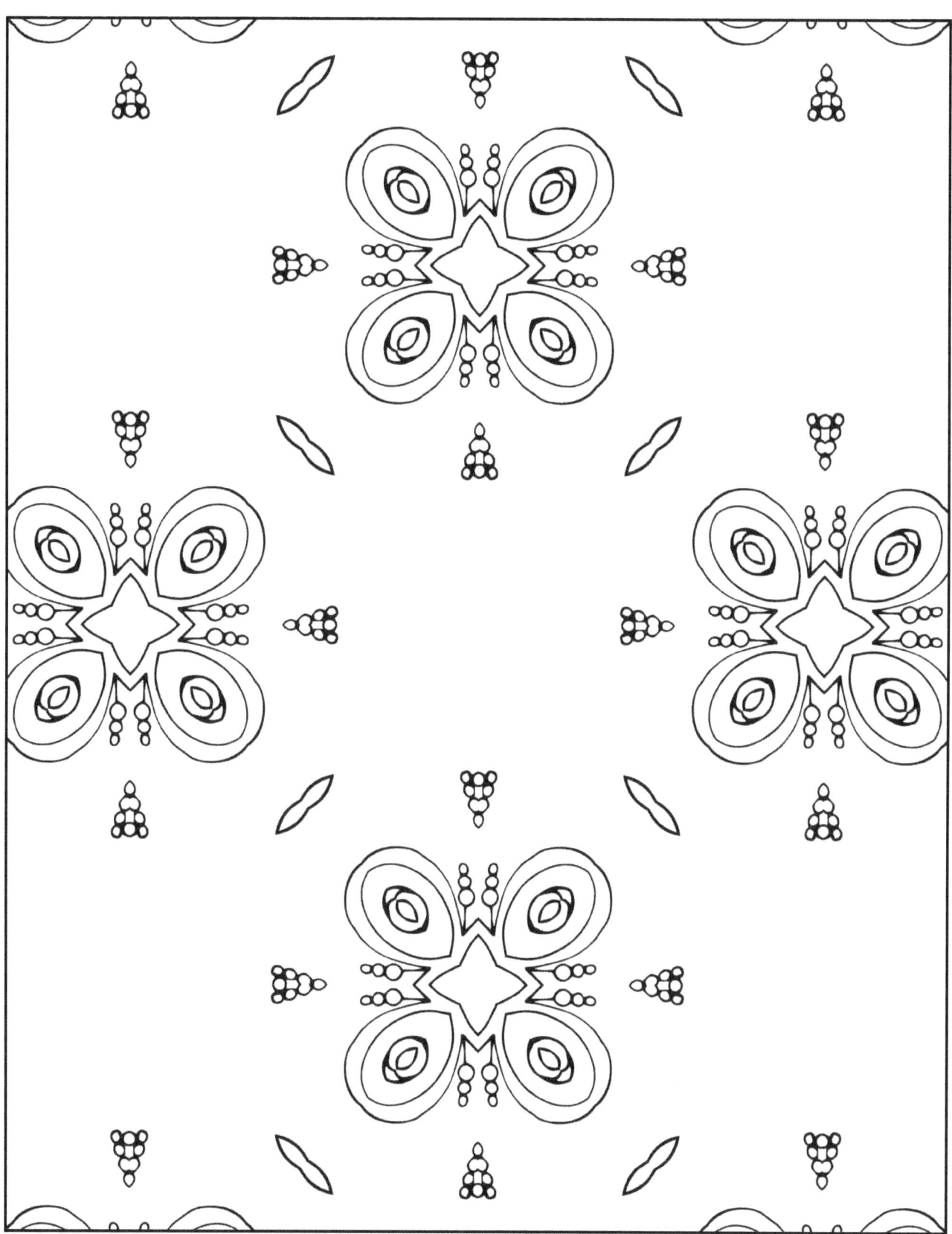

Notes

Notes

Blotter Page

Two blotter pages have been included for your convenience. Remove one or both and use them as a barrier between the page you are coloring and the next.

The designs in this book have been printed on one side of the page, but markers often bleed through even the best paper. To keep your art work pristine as you color and create, use another piece of paper as a buffer between the pages of this book, or use a thin piece of cardboard (cut one side from a cereal box, or use the thin cardboard insert that is found inside a new shirt)

Blotter Page

Two blotter pages have been included for your convenience. Remove one or both and use them as a barrier between the page you are coloring and the next.

The designs in this book have been printed on one side of the page, but markers often bleed through even the best paper. To keep your art work pristine as you color and create, use another piece of paper as a buffer between the pages of this book, or use a thin piece of cardboard (cut one side from a cereal box, or use the thin cardboard insert that is found inside a new shirt)

Thank you for buying a MandaLove Coloring Book!

♥

We've put together a FREE Bonus package of new mandalas, available for you to download at this link:

www.MandaLovePress.com

♥

Join us on Facebook and take part in coloring contests and free book and supply give-aways. Show us your completed designs!

Facebook.com/CreativeColoringBooks

♥

Look for our coloring books on Amazon and at your local bookstore!

www.MyColorBooks.com

♥

Thank you for leaving a book review!

♥

Copyright © 2015 by Creative Coloring Books for Adults and MandaLove Press. All Rights Reserved. This publication is protected by copyright law. Please respect the law. No part of this publication may be reproduced, reused, republished, or distributed in any form or by any means, electronic or mechanical, or stored in a database or retrieval system without prior written permission from the artist and publisher.

www.ingramcontent.com/pod-product-compliance
Lightning Source LLC
Chambersburg PA
CBHW081015040426
42444CB00014B/3218